COMING INTO THE LIGHT

An Invitation

Photography by *Barrie Rolleston Cannon* and *George Cannon*

Barrie L. Cannon

George Cannon

Voyager Publications, Inc.   Atlanta, Georgia

To our parents for their
love and support

We gratefully acknowledge permission from the publishers to quote from the following sources:

from A WALK THROUGH THE YEAR by Edwin Way Teale. Copyright © 1978 by Edwin Way Teale. Reprinted by permission of Dodd, Mead & Co., Inc., Publishers.

from THE MODERN TEMPER by Joseph Wood Krutch, Copyright © 1929 by Harcourt Brace Jovanovich, Inc.; copyright © 1957 by Joseph Wood Krutch. Reprinted by permission of Harcourt Brace Jovanovich, Inc., Publishers.

from THE OUTERMOST HOUSE by Henry Beston, Copyright © 1928, 1949, © 1956 by Henry Beston. Copyright © 1977 by Elizabeth C. Beston. Reprinted by permission of Holt, Rinehart and Winston, Publishers.

Quotes by Henry David Thoreau are from THE JOURNALS OF HENRY DAVID THOREAU and THE MAINE WOODS.

Quotes by Ralph Waldo Emerson are from a variety of Emerson's essays. The majority were reproduced as found in THE SELECTED WORKS OF RALPH WALDO EMERSON, The Modern Library Edition, Copyright © 1940, 1950, renewed 1968 by Random House, Inc.

This book was printed in Boston, Massachusetts by The Nimrod Press on 100 lb. Mead Black & White dull coated stock.

The design is by Doerr Associates of Arlington, Mass. The type is Palatino set by Typographic House of Boston. The color separations were made on a laser scanner by Color Prep of Cambridge, Mass.

We would like to express our gratitude to the people at Voyager Publications, The Nimrod Press, Doerr Associates, Color Prep, Boris Color Labs, and to Dave Egan, Chuck Moffatt, Roger Moore, Mark Braunsdorf, Neil and Virginia Croom, and Addie Spencer, and to all those who lent their time, advice, and support to this project. We thank you all.

Library of Congress Card Catalog No.: 79-65854   ISBN-0-9603020-0-X

The Invitation

"Like the wind, a brook exists only through motion. Down the narrow groove it has worn in the earth, hurrying toward the greater valleys of the rivers that will carry it to the sea, all the dark water foaming and gurgling below me rushes away into the night. The stream flows on and on. So the long life of the ever-renewing brook extends through the years. But it continues without awareness, without sensation, without emotion. Its existence is one of action, of music, of beauty; but it is life without life. The great gift of our lives is the gift of awareness."

— Edwin Way Teale

All too often in this world we have made for ourselves, ruled by schedules, time clocks, and deadlines, we lose sight of the true enduring scale of time, that of Nature. Her cadence and rhythm beat with the regularity of our own hearts, ignorant to our insensitivity, unaware of our self-imposed structure and rigidity. Daily we allow ourselves to be schooled by television networks and scheduled by unseen computers. We scan electrons with powerful microscopes and distant space with giant telescopic ears, searching for answers to the unknown or some communication from worlds beyond our comprehension. But we are like Mr. Teale's brook, proceeding toward an end without awareness, without sensation or emotion, looking toward tomorrow, unaware of today.

In making a place for mankind we have elevated ourselves beyond the realm of the natural world. We have isolated ourselves from our evolution. It has become popular today to search for the roots of our heritage yet we ignore the very genesis and origin of our existence in nature.

The invitation we extend to you through this book is one of reacquaintance and revival. By sharing with you some brief moments in our own experience, and the borrowed words of a few eloquent and sensitive authors, we hope to stir within you some curiosity, some need. We hope to kindle within you a desire to know the beauty of nature that lies so close around you. It is yours for the meager exchange of a few moments spent with open eyes and receptive mind.

It has not been necessary for us to venture far to find the beauty that is pictured here. The splendors of nature are not hidden in the recesses of the wilderness, nor reserved solely for the adventurous and physically strong, but are revealed in the parks and paths and roadsides that you pass every day. We have seen it only because we have allowed ourselves to. By viewing nature through the camera's lens we have become detached spectators, an audience to a grand production. The commonplace has become spectacle and nature has become phenomenon.

This is not to say that to be a photographer is to be made aware, nor is it necessary to capture nature to enjoy it. Nature cannot be captured in a two-dimensional page, but is felt and understood and enjoyed through the love of its existence. Our hope is that your experience of nature will not end with the closing of this cover, but that it will begin here.

"Nature and books belong to the eyes that see them."

— Ralph Waldo Emerson

"The production of a work of art throws a light upon the mystery of humanity. A work of art is an abstract or epitome of the world. It is the result or expression of nature, in miniature. For although the works of nature are innumerable and all different, the result or the expression of them all is similar and single. Nature is a sea of forms radically alike and even unique. A leaf, a sunbeam, a landscape, the ocean, make an analogous impression on the mind. What is common to them all—that perfectness and harmony, is beauty."

—Ralph Waldo Emerson

From Highway 73, St. Huberts, N.Y.

"...The difference between landscape and landscape is small, but there is great difference in the beholders. There is nothing so wonderful in any particular landscape as the necessity of being beautiful under which every landscape lies. Nature cannot be surprised in undress. Beauty breaks in everywhere."

— Ralph Waldo Emerson

Parker River National Wildlife Refuge,
Plum Island, Mass.

"What shall we do with a man who is afraid of the woods, their solitude and darkness? What salvation is there for him? God is silent and mysterious."

— Henry David Thoreau

Cummings Nature Center, Naples, N.Y.

*"Talk of mysteries! Think of our life in nature—
daily to be shown matter, to come in contact with
it—rocks, trees, wind on our cheeks! The solid
earth! The actual world! The common sense!
Contact! Contact! Who are we? Where are we?"*

—Henry David Thoreau

Hancock St., Lexington, Mass.

"Undoubtedly we have no questions to ask which are unanswerable. We must trust the perfection of the creation so far as to believe that whatever curiosity the order of things has awakened in our minds, the order of things can satisfy."

— Ralph Waldo Emerson

Cascade Pond Trail, Blue Mountain Lake, N.Y.

"Nature will bear the closest inspection. She invites us to lay our eye level with her smallest leaf, and take an insect view of its plain."

— Henry David Thoreau

New England Wildflower Society,
Framingham, Mass.

"How cunningly nature hides every wrinkle of her inconceivable antiquity under roses and violets and morning dew!"

— *Ralph Waldo Emerson*

Hancock St., Lexington, Mass.

"Each humblest plant, or weed, as we call it, stands there to express some thought or mood of ours, and yet how long it stands in vain!"

—Henry David Thoreau

Great Meadows
National Wildlife Refuge,
Concord, Mass.

"God, the Great Giver, can open the whole universe to our gaze in the narrow space of a single lane."

— Rabandranath Tagore

*Wachusett Meadows
Wildlife Sanctuary,
Princeton, Mass.*

"We shall see but little way if we require to understand what we see. How few things can a man measure with the tape of his understanding! How many greater things might he be seeing in the meanwhile!"

— Henry David Thoreau

Great Meadows National Wildlife Refuge,
Concord, Mass.

"Whatever aid is to be derived from the use of a scientific term, we can never begin to see anything as it is so long as we remember the scientific term which always our ignorance has imposed on it. Natural objects and phenomena are in this sense forever wild and unnamed by us."

— Henry David Thoreau

Robert H. Treman State Park,
Ithaca, N.Y.

"…With all your science can you tell how
it is, and whence it is, that light comes into
the soul?…"

—Henry David Thoreau

Cummings Nature Center, Naples, N.Y.

*"It is the marriage of the soul with Nature
that makes the intellect fruitful, and gives birth
to imagination."*

—Henry David Thoreau

Great Meadows National Wildlife Refuge,
Concord, Mass.

"…Nature abhors a vacuum, and if I can only walk with sufficient carelessness I am sure to be filled."

— Henry David Thoreau

Great Meadows
National Wildlife Refuge,
Concord, Mass.

"You must converse much with the field and woods, if you would imbibe such health into your mind and spirit as you covet for your body."

— Henry David Thoreau

Bedford St., Lexington, Mass.

"Nature is a mutable cloud, which is always and never the same."

— *Ralph Waldo Emerson*

Parker River National Wildlife Refuge,
Plum Island, Mass.

"You must love the crust of the earth on which you dwell more than the sweet crust of any bread or cake. You must be able to extract nutriment out of a sand-heap. You must have so good an appetite as this, else you will live in vain."

—Henry David Thoreau

Parker River National Wildlife Refuge,
Plum Island, Mass.

"…There is nothing inorganic. This earth is not, then, a mere fragment of dead history, strata upon strata, like the leaves of a book, an object for a museum and an antiquarian, but living poetry, like the leaves of a tree, —not a fossil earth, but a living specimen…."

—Henry David Thoreau

Ravenswood Park, Magnolia, Mass.

"Nature never makes haste; her systems revolve at an even pace. The buds swell imperceptibly, without hurry or confusion, as though the short spring days were an eternity. Why, then, should man hasten as if anything less than eternity were allotted for the least deed?"

—Henry David Thoreau

New England Wildflower Society, Framingham, Mass.

"Every part of nature teaches that the passing away of one life is the making of room for another. The oak dies down to the ground, leaving within its rind a virgin mould, which will impart a vigorous life to an infant forest."

— Henry David Thoreau

Cascade Pond Trail,
Blue Mountain Lake, N.Y.

"Nature, in her blind thirst for life, has filled every possible cranny of the rotting earth with some sort of fantastic creature."

— Joseph Wood Krutch

Robert H. Treman State Park, Ithaca, N.Y.

"Into every empty corner, into all forgotten things and nooks, Nature struggles to pour life, pouring life into the death, life into life itself."

—Henry Beston

Castle Rock Trail,
Blue Mountain Lake, N.Y.

51

"…They that waved so loftily, how contentedly they return to dust again and are laid low, resigned to lie and decay at the foot of the tree and afford nourishment to new generations of their kind, as well as to flutter on high! How they are mixed up, all species, — oak and maple and chestnut and birch! They are about to add a leaf's breadth to the depth of the soil. We are all the richer for their decay. Nature is not cluttered with them. She is a perfect husbandman; she stores them all."

— Henry David Thoreau

Cascade Pond Trail, Blue Mountain Lake, N.Y.

"...Surrounded by our thoughts or imaginary objects, living in our ideas, not one in a million ever sees the objects which are actually around him."

— Henry David Thoreau

Cascade Pond Trail, Blue Mountain Lake, N.Y.

"The visible marks of extraordinary wisdom and power appear so plainly in all the works of creation that a rational creature who will but seriously reflect on them cannot miss the discovery of a deity."

—John Locke

Highland Park, Rochester, N.Y.

"The energy of nature is displayed in the smallest things and in the smallest things lies excellence of art."

— *Algarotti*

New England Wildflower Society,
Framingham, Mass.

59

"I feel a little alarmed when it happens that I have walked a mile into the woods bodily, without getting there in spirit....What business have I in the woods, if I am thinking of something out of the woods?..."

—Henry David Thoreau

Cummings Nature Center,
Naples, N.Y.

"Each phase of nature, while not invisible, is yet not too distinct and obtrusive. It is there to be found when we look for it, but not demanding our attention...."

—Henry David Thoreau

Chapel Pond, St. Huberts, N.Y.

"When you think that your walk is profitless and a failure, and you can hardly persuade yourself not to return, it is on the point of being a success, for then you are in that subdued and knocking mood to which Nature never fails to open."

—Henry David Thoreau

Cascade Pond Trail, Blue Mountain Lake, N.Y.

"...It is only necessary to behold thus the least fact or phenomenon, however familiar, from a point a hair's breadth aside from our habitual path or routine, to be overcome, enchanted by its beauty and significance...."

—Henry David Thoreau

Minnow Pond Trail, Blue Mountain Lake, N.Y.

"I now descend round the corner of the grain-field, through the pitch pine wood into a lower field, more inclosed by woods, and find myself in a colder, damp and misty atmosphere, with much dew on the grass. I seem to be nearer to the origin of things.... An atmosphere which has forgotten the sun, where the ancient principle of moisture prevails. It is laden with the condensed fragrance of plants and, as it were, distilled in dews."

— Henry David Thoreau

Off Highway 64, Highlands, N.C.

"I walk over the hills, to compare great things with small, as through a gallery of pictures, ever and anon looking through a gap in the wood, as through the frame of a picture, to a more distant wood or hillside, painted with several more coats of air...."

— Henry David Thoreau

Cummings Nature Center, Naples, N.Y.

"...—then at eve the sun goes down westward, and the wind goes down with it, and the dews begin to purify the air and make it transparent, and the lakes and rivers acquire a glassy stillness, reflecting the skies, the reflex of the day.... The attractive point is that line where the water meets the land, not distinct, but known to exist...."

—Henry David Thoreau

Great Meadows National Wildlife Refuge,
Concord, Mass.

"A field of water betrays the spirit that is in the air. It has new life and motion. It is intermediate between land and sky. On land, only the grass and trees wave, but the water itself is rippled by the wind. I see the breeze dash across it in streaks and flakes of light. It is somewhat singular that we should look down on the surface of water. We shall look down on the surface of air next, and mark where a still subtler spirit sweeps over it...."

—Henry David Thoreau

From Highway 30
near Tupper Lake, N.Y.

"...I wish so to live ever as to derive my satisfactions and inspirations from the commonest events, every-day phenomena, so that what my senses hourly perceive, my daily walk, the conversation of my neighbors, may inspire me, and I may dream of no heaven but that which lies about me...."

—Henry David Thoreau

Great Meadows National Wildlife Refuge,
Concord, Mass.

"…All this you will see, and much more, if you are prepared to see it, — if you look for it….We do not realize how far and widely, or how near and narrowly, we are to look. The greater part of the phenomena of nature are for this reason concealed to us all our lives…."

—Henry David Thoreau

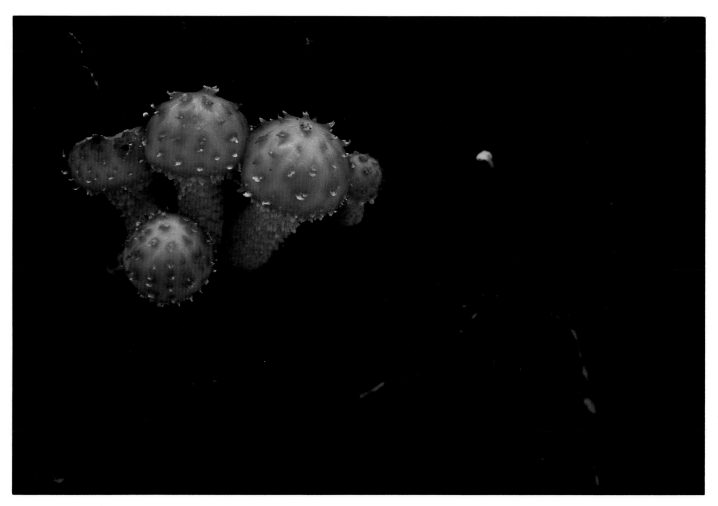

Cascade Pond Trail, Blue Mountain Lake, N.Y.

"…These sunset clouds, these delicately emerging stars, with their private and ineffable glances, signify it and proffer it. I am taught the poorness of our invention, the ugliness of towns and palaces. Art and luxury have early learned that they must work as enhancement and sequel to this original beauty…."

— *Ralph Waldo Emerson*

Blue Mountain Lake, Blue Mountain Lake, N.Y.

"…He who knows the most; he who knows what sweets and virtues are in the ground, the waters, the plants, the heavens, and how to come at these enchantments, is the rich and royal man…."

— *Ralph Waldo Emerson*

Wachusett Meadows Wildlife Sanctuary,
Princeton, Mass.

*"…Nature does not cast pearls before swine.
There is just as much beauty visible to us in the
landscape as we are prepared to appreciate, —not
a grain more. The actual objects which one person will see from a particular hill top are just as
different from those which another will see as the
persons are different….We cannot see anything
until we are possessed with the idea of it, and
then we can hardly see anything else…."*

—Henry David Thoreau

Robert H. Treman State Park, Ithaca, N.Y.

"Simply to see a distant horizon through a clear air, — the fine outline of a distant hill or a blue mountain-top through some new vista, — this is wealth enough for one afternoon."

—Henry David Thoreau

View from Little Yellow Mountain, Highlands, N.C.

"…'Nature is not fixed but fluid. Spirit alters, moulds, makes it. The immobility or bruteness of nature is the absence of spirit; to pure spirit it is fluid, it is volatile, it is obedient. Every spirit builds itself a house, and beyond its house a world, and beyond its world a heaven. Know then that the world exists for you….'"

— Ralph Waldo Emerson

Bostwick Road, Ithaca, N.Y.

"Come forth into the light of things, let Nature be your teacher."

— Wordsworth

Blue Mountain Lake, Blue Mountain Lake, N.Y.

PHOTOGRAPHERS NOTE: Because of our interest in producing a book that would illustrate the beauty of nature that we all might share, our images have come from areas accessible, in most instances, to the average person. Some were taken on our own street, many in our own or adjacent communities, most within a day's drive of our home in Lexington, Massachusetts. These types of scenes are not restricted to the areas in which they were taken, but could be found just as easily in the woods, or parks, or sanctuaries nearest your own home.

The equipment we use is fairly simple. All but a few images were photographed on Kodachrome 64 film under existing light. We use Minolta 35mm cameras and a variety of lenses, but primarily the 21mm, 50mm macro, 100mm macro, and 75-200mm zoom lenses.

Barrie Rolleston Cannon grew up in Atlanta, Georgia. She holds a B.A. degree from Birmingham Southern College in painting and art history, and studied photography at Rochester Institute of Technology in Rochester, New York. She is also the former co-owner of The Living Image, an Atlanta photography gallery and workshop facility.

George Cannon grew up in Decatur, Georgia. He has worked at a variety of jobs including land surveying, mechanic, auto shop manager, and warehouseman. He is a self-taught photographer and an accomplished artist in stained glass.

The photographer/authors currently reside and work in Ithaca, . New York.